I0224263

Some Perfect Year

Cameron Gearen

Some Perfect Year

Shearsman Books

First published in the United Kingdom in 2016 by
Shearsman Books
50 Westons Hill Drive
Emersons Green
BRISTOL
BS16 7DF

Shearsman Books Ltd Registered Office
. 30–31 St. James Place, Mangotsfield, Bristol BS16 9JB
(this address not for correspondence)

www.shearsman.com

ISBN 978-1-84861-484-0

Copyright © Cameron Gearen, 2016.
The right of Cameron Gearen to be identified as the author
of this work has been asserted by her in accordance with the
Copyrights, Designs and Patents Act of 1988.
All rights reserved.

Contents

For Cleo and Iris.
Take my lantern for your piecework.
And for John and Ann Gearen
with love and gratitude.

Nocturne

To stir would be to slip—
To look would be to drop—[…]

Seed—summer—tomb—
Whose Doom to whom?

from 'A Pit—but Heaven over it—'
Emily Dickinson

Invitation

Come with stones and a selectively green car.

I've set aside a weekend for crying and sleeping.

You weren't there when I stretched the laundry crossways.

Wishing a homestead, wailing like that hound.

Doors sound like airplanes taking off.

If I thought you were listening, love.

She ledged herself until they came to get her.

She talked like stroll was a word she liked.

I hated the room's corner: intimate.

I learned night is a lamp to turn off, lasts.

City, erase me. Mail me stamped and worn.

Body knows the slow stall into long night's sleep.

The table yawns between us.

Neat lines grade my page gray.

I beg you to calculate the burnish hue.

She had a fine haircut but her teeth were stained.

We're out of dish soap. I terrible and I wish.

Aerial not the fountain's best view.

If I thought you were listening, love.

I'll be standing in line at the post office.

Come by if you want to see me.

Fun with Dying

The year you died was gala festive. Didn't I party dress for monthly
plane flights from my lake to your ocean? Each time you gauntly
greeted, your skin poked carbon blue where needles entered, the strange

shunt dangle from its temporary home, you St. Sebastian and your arrows.
Your girl and I ate out and brought you cheese. We tooled Seattle
like tourists, its single rainless winter we sequined, brought you

accordioned nosegays. You seemed to like hospital sleeping, fluttering
nurses to morphine drip. Sometimes we restauranted sans you.
You loved to see us glow and we obliged. Layers peeled you papery,

trapeze-artist light, your fingernails gone to skin. The drugs took your hair
and left you seal-smooth; carved chin to chisel, lashless eyes, the shell melting
and your warm core soaking sheets, turning toward the grisly plants

we windowsilled. We shopped that city, found expensive knits, boutique
sweaters with slate buttons. We bought eyeliner by the tub. Your girl,
she held my hand while yours skeletoned. *Nothing* you said when we asked

what gifts. I zipped my knee-high boots, she fastened her trench, breezed
out. We always smelled of apricot scrub, avocado. Why would someone stay
bedside, listen to a rattle? Rattles come from coughs and lead to comas.

We weren't the knitting type, we had exhausted crosswords. It was you
who urged us *go*, a day not circumscribe our wantings. We wished you well
again and burly but turned your sick ghoulish. The doc and residents
       predicted

nine more months—a long time in my short life. *Let's go, he wants us to,*
I told her and we left you again, bright things to be bought, a turquoise scarf
my neck needed, crème brulée I loved to its caramel end. You lay

thirty-nine mixed years quilted on your rotten body: thought things through.
Set the pillows, rode the angles, fresh from your sponge bath. You
knew the shift change rhythm like a poker hand. Nightcap nurse

took your vitals and we dropped off a confection. When months ticked
        through
to April, we all agreed it had been a beautiful year and a fine one for dying in.
No one could say when a starless Washington winter had glimmered so.

[sketch]

or flu can burn   *sound*   through a house
this pale one   not the black   next farm
eight miles   they said black soil black
painted earth   horse and buggy my great-
grandfather but   *it's a neat sound*   black
soil   let's build on it   horse and buggy
neat doctor *neat* evening *neat* piano
my grandmother age five then or six
neat sound   she had been to the henhouse
pair of shoes only for that   couldn't reach
was her father ill   the flu burned
through this pale house   painted black
sun magnet fertile like soil   *sound*
as in neat   outside found soil/corn/silo
ears they fed the pigs   pair of shoes
for walking in chicken shit   shoes dumped
crusted in the mud room   doctors
made house calls   nowhere for that flu
to sound   no host victim carrier
for eight miles round so it killed him   1918
then grounded   drying rack for bodies   city
apartments a day's ride away   Chicago
left his family itchy   wife expecting the fourth
neat sound sound sound   rattle   wheel
or a rooster   but only him   there weren't
any neighbors to speak of   to infect
corn mostly   some soy   some tobacco
in Chicago some stayed alive
to carry   corpses four flights down
she watched her daddy's   body roll away
in the hearse   remembers how the horses
strained silent under   the coffin's weight

Local Attraction

Barbed wire knot I know your worthy
hitch. Visit beautiful Sundown,
where oil wells seek gold. Burrs
invest embed my sock jeans boot
skin. I think if they stop fighting,
my father and his girlfriend, the one
who leaves her wadded panties
behind the door. For what exactly
did I fly here besides the grown-ups
said? But they've boozed
since morning Bloody Marys,
handing off their vodka-soaked
celery sticks to me, laughing
too loud at Kotex commercials,
now driving this barren grid
past the cotton gin's buzz, past
the cemetery, to Sundown,
a curiosity. I can't
get their attention. Crouched
between tumbleweeds, lodged
on red dirt where nothing
grows, I'm picking burrs
from my own ankles. I
can do this. Sometimes
I clean their dingy panhandle
ranch house, babysit her hungry
girls. I could make you an omelet,
bring it to you in bed. In June
I'll be ten. His morning coffee
drowns what sweetness. Summers
like this I grow up sleeping
on the green velveteen couch,
rubbed bare where my knees
seek a groove.

Compounded

Hanging lamps dangle over no table.

Witch hazel hands. When the child was small.

You know the list. It starts with silk.

Blind TV shouts Mandarin.

Rubble lot, transport me.

We stack suitcases like popsicles: red green pink.

A place is an envelope for memory.

Like blisters, the inside manifests.

Rust can orange and brown and cut open.

I drip water over American coffee.

We'll give you the hero's welcome.

My little slice of heaven: the stinking downstairs store.

The body hiccoughing flamboyance, buoyancy.

The courtyard shows foresight.

Stitching on a red slipper.

Burgeon is a word about growth.

Tingle itch swarm the window.

Cities matter mightily and I'm in one.

Where's my ladder, means of egress?

What you say is whole my mortar.

Skin poison to the edge of membrane.

Colored newsprint rubs my hands solid.

Buzzered gate: tip the guards.

You say arrive.

You stand in the window and say arrive.

Right to Remain

Did I ask him, chase me off the métro
up the worn slick stairs? My profligate self

nineteen in Paris. Boulevard Raspail,
my door's hydraulic slo-mo close threatens

death. Two feet, legs, torso, shoulders, head: he's in
he's in the key the key. I smell him.

My hair still wet from the pool. The concierge
where? fuck these tiles, these mute cornices

no one home.

Door number two, glib-red and craven, its knocker polished.
must / get / behind behind behind

open, SLAM, fumble, lock, *thank god I'll live*
and I pant with my back to it. Cut.

My profligate self set my Aqua-Net "do"
on fire lighting a cigarette in the thin blue circle

of a stove burner. It didn't burn. Turned

from hair to ash without flame and lay
like sawdust on the stovetop.

Did I ask him, please undress
here on this boat launch? Even the heron

scissor-walked to shadow. I stayed. *Be polite.*
Miguel from Mexico slid closer, opened a beer,

lit a joint. *Lest he think I'm racist. Or a prude.*
Held me hostage, swimsuited on an upended kayak

in the gathering dusk. *In Spanish
your name's an aphrodisiac*, he said.

Then chanted it.

Parisienne uniform: Burberry plaid scarf
and matching raincoat, umbrella optional.

My French roommate, a law student,
called me a target in my American running shoes.
Tar-zhay. She said, *It's no surprise they honk.*

My French roommate said, *If you ride the métro
with your hair wet from the pool everyone will know
you're American. We don't do this. We dry our hair.
What did you expect?*

Despised and this proof: the box of garbage
delivered to my doorstep one Sunday morning.

I'm twenty-one and studious. The cruelest part
the red red bow. Touching, inviting. *For me?*

Its insides rank and rotten. *For me?*
My roommate's pallor, my false bravado.

I'm despicable and my ex a lunatic.
Receiving garbage renders me garbage.

My profligate self dared

buy a fuchsia wool skirt on the Boul Mich.
Wore flats all winter until chilblained.

The tennis court snow-logged and numb,

me the only mittenless one, always
that bright flag ending at my knees.

I dream my husband's African friend rapes me.

Reverend, I'm reverent. Cajoles, at first.
Bright kitchen. Folds my body

from behind and desecrates.

Dream screws my jaw tight and wakes me,
achy, at dawn. I never should have told

(them). It's too like

life. Defies description.

[flight 312]

seconding with the effort   it's tight
in here   excuse   this blue-eyed
bald baby I'm holding   the aisle's scant

hips and thighs   here's an alcove here's
scant in the kitchen   spatulaed
No Mom my daughter writes   flies her note

toward me and it obeys laws of earth-physics
not flotation   we're bubbled   southwest
to get around through the edge   excuse me, blue-eyed

baby   someone should fuss   fuss over
fuss about   touch a white-shirted back
strangers   scant   landing gear lets down

like milk   hours the rocky range   window ago
retract your bulky halo   to get by
like a cocktail party   he's come casual

a portal porthole   we're in it fill it wad the pillow
stretch   seconding with the effort
I'm holding a blue-eyed baby   stratospheric

strangers   my daughter's note   nosedives
toward carpet   I stoop to read it   *No Mom*
put that other lady's baby   down

Diurnal

Sunday wakes me like a wasp's nest.

Either it's a checklist or it's a quilted dome.

Remember the look of the worn daisy?

I threaten its papery quiet all day.

You are my symptom and I love you.

Eggplant expands in the frying oil.

The hopefulness of children behind us.

Do you understand how a turkey roosts?

Hives turned my ankles shiny.

I'm the one in the video who drops and drops her fork.

It's the nighttime wearing of the light-up crown.

You patient offered hot water, lotion.

I'm going to lie here and miss my mother.

Hunkered big to their smallish branch.

Sleep all day till the house stirs.

Daughter, you look radiant at the stove.

What Water Divides

To dig a grave in coral
takes all week by hand.
I see miles: west weather
skims the bluff, the frigatebirds
near land. My daughter
spins, up nights cart-
wheeling. When she hides—
her joke—I'm not ready. I scan
and scan waves, surf, rocks
for her black mermaid hair,
for the float and bob her limbs
might do, a flail a ripple.
Graves make strange cribs,
picket-fenced, and cousins bring
plastic flowers from Marsh Harbour's
Variety. Last night, hermit crabs
scarfed scraps she left the cat.
She said, *Sunlight*
waters my eyes. I know
the sodden brown body we pulled
to the beach once, a girl not dead
but worse, lost too long,
would not start third grade
that fall or any.
Pumped her thin chest.
Slapped her; she lay still.
Hundred stairs I ran to the phone.
Her grave a haven. The Caribbean
devours sailor fathers, cholera
rots mothers, these buried babies
weren't safe and mine are barely.
I bugle her name in the knee-high grass
that stung her foot. See her
face down, a small dark spot

where the reef begins. I could carry
her hair in a locket, wear
my hands thin from wringing.
I drag her giggling from the closet.
They say a mother once walked
into waves and her baby starved
or died of grief on dry land. See
her hem spread? See her stumble?

red

wedding lollipop flame color pack your heart in boxes and   ship them
via eighteen-wheeler   red hankie red flag red hat red slogan   it's what
we wear our blood vessels for   look in any eye and document the
spread   an inside climb we careful stall   it blooms when meets oxygen
an earth a very alive   carve from a vein this or that ruby   does the
color resent being championed   its symbolization   no talk of shade
or variation   tomato strawberry crabapple   all of which have been
known to   present and turn   an inner pale a getting at what it means
red can be shined can be valorized   perhaps beyond deserving   *hong*
in Chinese   a name worthy of daughters   a shade outside the orbit of
a swan

Proverb

If you find a young rabbit's carcass on your steps,
hind paws leaking into cement, call your landlord

who will tell you, sure, borrow his shovel but beyond that
he can't help. If you find a rat, don't take it

for a possum. One is gray; the other has a long, stiff tail.
The fox who killed it slinks, is always slinking, away

under the myrtle. In the house, you are looking under
things. Even in the cupboard, dry cornmeal streaks

the shelf, overturned glass a home for winter hornets.
Food moths spiral, drunk on rice husk. One is stuck

to the trap, flapping. You don't have to lift
the glass. Wings clatter. Things aren't all bad.

Two handsome key chains, right on your front steps.
Lucky? Inside: the phone, the landlord. Ants sprout

from the bathroom's cool tile. In the mirror, your face:
a chrysanthemum that might thrust a stamen out,

petals like bunched brown cotton, green-stemmed neck.
Wings brush the walls of the glass. Rats glower;

possums waddle: that's the difference between them.
If the hornet were a firefly, he'd be a lighthouse

on your steps warning animals—winged, hoofed, pawed—
of danger: narrow straits, shallow channel.

Many-Windowed House

Greta Daubs Solvent

This is about a house. Says Tertullian of Carthage,
To widowhood signed and sealed before the Lord
nought is necessary but perseverance. Where wall
pulls away from wall: plaster, spackle. Prime
and paint: *lilypad*, what remains of a gallon
they bought for the girls' room. Nought
is necessary. Where the pipe burst, heal
the warped wood. It will drink mineral oil.
And for the living, build a root cellar
to save mossy things. How to fashion
a potato coffin where no eyes will sprout.
Signed and sealed. Dank, dank, like a monument
in the room's middle so air may circulate. Persevere.
Hurry to plait the girls' hair in the bright kitchen.

Greta Wears the Morning

Greta's sadness sewn on the bias. De-nuded,
which means to make un-nude or to clothe.
In somber cloak. To have the same black dress—
crenelated—fashioned every other spring.
What became of her shoe collection?
This is about a house, their first rental. On the water.
What's poignant in youth leaves the middle-aged
dredged like a fryer, towel-dried. To think
she painted the paneling bright, coaxed annuals
in her windowbox, grew full. O where
is our seaside getaway, replete
with tidal pools? Where the rocky low-tide
path to Eagle Cay, its pink
and many-windowed house?

After Terrific Effort, Greta

Should she frontier and homestead, then, tame
the yard he loved, mulch the roots, weed
the beds, thin the morning glories?
From her window, forsythia: its purpose
and intention. It would cross the yard,
send shoots up the opposite fence. And so
she wears through gloves. Thinks: I will plant
a sugar maple to be tapped some early spring
when all underfoot cracks brittle.

For the pruning, she gets estimates. One says,
Daytime phone? Says, *Oh you want me to
PRUNE your TREE*?
Greta: Does my widow-voice, faint
at the end of a wire, advertise loss?

Greta Makes an Offering

Her wheezing midnight husband huddled
his tight lungs in steam's path, pot on low
boil and a hand towel like hair
to his shoulders. She cut ginger, swaddled
and mummified. She made for him a poultice—
clay, fenugreek, camphor—and on his freckled back
mounded it. Press each dry seed—not enough oil
on this earth to anoint him.

               Widows see where fresh water
empties into salt. The literal mouth also estuary.
Her boot crunch in the marsh grass,
its scratchy grab at her leg. Can name
his shorebirds: killdeer, piper, bufflehead, gull.
Can trace Great Blue Heron, brown where it blends
to brown coral.

Interlude: Widow's Menu

Cookies: lacy or cakey.

Chicken: staunch-stuffed

or with-a-kick. Meat

packs a wallop.

Butter: Dollop or pat.

Don't call the haricots

green beans; it's common.

Don't call the pigeon

oiseau. Don't leak

secrets. Sauté, braise.

Chitlins or dirty rice?

Whatever you're having.

Greta Like a Plucked String

Had said to him: Today, plan our dotage, Love,
not the RV but the land we'll bruise and love
to fruit. Stain the grape arbor, grade the meadow.
Bet on longevity. Bet, in fact, on infinity. Dotage
in which I dote, you dote, old/blind/numb. Argue:
was the grouse ruffled or ruffed. You will make for me
bread pudding flambé. Soak crumbs in rum
and crows scavenge bones.

                    Storms, she dreamed his death—
deck's raucous pitch, spray and his sputtering end.
Soon the funeral, the myrtled yard. The watered
house plants seep into wood, musty circles she scrubs
and soothes. Clothesline creaks on its pulleys.
She would make a paper flower and water it religiously,
rake and rake. Leaf caught in her braid: collage.

Greta Thwarts the Id

Greta dreams a fusty hall lined with monographs.
Reads a cracking volume and learns: were she Bedouin
and also ancient, she would pass, once widowed,
to the husband's male agnate, a brother.

She will shave her icicle hair, gorgeous
and alarming hat. She will sweep her tent
neat and neater. What textures this world?
Figs, camels, heat, sand—all she knows of it

a PBS special. He is expansive when liquored.
To her tent he steals and finds her bald,
no bangles. Does he rage? Retreat?
Does he take what's owed him?

I don't shimmer, murmur, rustle, shine.
Love, you are luminescent, orb and sky.

Greta Gives Good Advice

Husk the widow, find a naked ear. Silk
drifts sticky skyline-wards. Late summer,
put up peaches: the skin, once blanched,
begs to be peeled, fruit glossy like an eyeball.

To the girls Greta says, Peel your eyes.
How can they, through heat-steamed glass,
see the ruby-throated hummingbird hover?
Plan dinner: something ground, with cumin.

Something slow to marinate, sure to ripen
and lose its flavor to splintered peppercorns.
For celery use fennel. Crack a caraway seed:
its soft meat poisons the broth. Greta corrals

the peaches, six to a jar. Plunges fruit in ice till
her hands mottle and her fingernails candle blue.

Jeremiad

I've never been to me.
I've never been <u>in</u> me.

But daily I rehearse
how I drowned.

from 'Self-Representation'
Liz Waldner

Flashback

This starting also an end
          (to not knowing).

                    A thing to know wrapped in
                    foil in my mind and how—
                    slowly— the talking cure
                    undid its crimped edges
                    until.

A Friday night in April
        my daughter called
her voice small as a pebble
at the line's end.

                Past nine already.

                Where are you calling from?

The bathroom
and the tiles elbowed her skin
bounced her voice around.

                Where are T's parents?

I don't know.

                Where is T?

I don't know.

                You sound scared. Want me
                to come and pick you up?

No.

Just her breathing, the way
a flower would
breathe if it had lungs.

> *Honey. Please let me come.*
> *If it's not fun, let's try another time.*

No. I want to stay.

But I'm
eating
my heart
by then.
Back
into
my chest,
I tell
its messy
walls and
ventricles.
Back.

> *Call if you change your mind.*

Ring off.

In my hand the receiver turns
to a bottle of my father's Vitabath,
circa 1974, and now I'm screaming
at what I see, what's escaped the foil
wrapper, not the Vitabath but its

sequel, this movie my mind stored
that I hope I'm making up? but can't
be as it's more graphic, fractured
and wholly itself than any celluloid
I've seen. I'm yelling for it to stop
but it won't and doesn't and my crying
hysteria also stored where that
movie came from, loud and rough
and bottomless, scaring A and
threatening to wake our youngest.
What I see, I believe and can't
at the same time: the ruined, rotten
tundra of my life. Get under, I think,
but A won't let me go to the bed's cavity.
A, he's raping me, he's hurting me,
he's trying to kill me and A says
Shhh, it's over but it doesn't feel
over to me. Sleep won't come and I
wonder if it will some other night. My
father is huge and finds me in my
wicker chest, his hand a vise on my
wrist. He smacks the paraphernalia
to the floor and sets himself on
my small body I now see from above.
And rewind. When freezing dawn
visits Connecticut, A and the little one
still sleeping upstairs, I know all is changed
and also not. Denial, that gauzy curtain,
lies torn. Meaning eludes me.
Ground-swell. Ice floe. My daughter
comes home tired but unscathed.
I'm the scathed one.

Amnesiac's Journal

I dream sugar cane. Dream brightness in busy rooms: I try and try to tell. Warthog. Rat. Something small I am, certainly killed.

Cry or drive or shoulder or crash or cry.

Go back to sleep; it's just a dream.

Flu fever stitch. Break-bone day.

Did you know you're bleeding here?

I'm so pretty love me
In this dress, stay late, sway
All the grown-up men
Magnetized
I have experience

First Bluebonnet's whole family died, I'm reading to my six-year-old. *All of them?*

The blank blank chunks I didn't think. Here a decade lost.

His hand expert at my larynx. He is a master: no bruises.

The resiliency gene
dormant until activated

by need. Two long
alleles, spun or straight.

Chairs I block
the door with
but he'll in.

The tragic accident of DNA. Chagrin, chagrin.

Count backwards from forty.
Chew or hold ice.
Suck ginger candy.
I'm here now.
Twenty-first century,
Connecticut.
Review French.
Circle all the gs on this page.
Have sex.
Snap a rubber band on my wrist.
Have sex.

Chrysalides the plural of chrysalis. I like a dictionary who yields her secrets.

My six-year-old thins, like a girl,
with teeth that urge the edge of babyhood.
In dreams she suckles where she never
did. Bluebonnet, she-who-is-alone, cried
for her lost parents, then painted the hillsides
with flowers. It's the same every
night, this story, what she wants from it.

A stench, an inside-outing.
He grabbed me, and I learned
(four-year-olds do) to pull
the skin taut. Wolf, sheep.

Is it possible to win the trauma group?

I fire the psychiatrist who
follows me into the hallway then parking lot
tells me my smile lights up the whole room.

Bikini wax is of this world. There's no spa
in Tartarus. How
do I get back there?

Despite everything, people have babies.

This heavy heavy thing. My kind
husband, in collapsed time, the cruel one.
Gone, I'm gone.
I can't hear him talking to me.

I am the woman who had devils in her and could not get them out.

My daughter loves a light-up turtle. A glowing bulb. A skating tutu.
Sequins. She grows while she sleeps. I check.

I will someday champion other things—maybe the merits of domestic apricots in fall. Some perfect year.

First her whole family died, the story says. Sadness there's no name for, she-who-is-alone. Then. You know which ones I mean, the little blue flowers? They stitch hillsides, light up even walls.

Hide-out, circa 1973

[His rage and its
Result. Lend me some
Dignity, walls. Cover
Your ears, bed.]

Do you know the closet's   insides he'll sleep it off my arm
Misbent   pins and needles throat sore where he seared it
My cells knitting   their latest split efficient   at it
Dark in here   I make out a suede handbag with fringe like

A mother might   wear someplace where shopping trips
Occur a purse that might signal optimism audacity   a market
Perhaps perhaps Woolworth's purse   from another world

There's no telling to tell I have to believe I can inhabit a sentence

Evacuee

I am her empty cornmeal tin.

It's uncanny quiet between my ears.

I fit in boxes of any sort.

Unthinking organs pump my blood.

If objects are not solid.

If objects are much too solid.

The heart speeds up and learns its death.

Amnesiac stare at my torn flesh.

(Now that I know.)

There's only one of us here.

His roaring also tears.

On no account look in his eyes.

I fit in the nexus of his fist.

To start with a heart broken.

To think evil normal.

A pattern emerged.

Between episodes I dragged my Barbies curbside.

Maybe a lucky lonely afternoon.

I'm waiting where he told me on the made bed.

Empty tin empty.

Sound is air forced from the abdomen.

Speech is the shape lips give it.

I learn long division.

Words don't string themselves.

Vocal cords for hire.

No matter how I tell this death.

This thin slow falling of the mind.

The cells store a sequence.

Truth floats outside language.

There's only one of us here.

Don't call survive another name.

That girl emerged torn.

Some stories defy telling.

Telling

That's when blindness set
in. Silent movie. I knew
all those door hinges, their
capacity for swivel. Ceded
my sight to the cornice's
stare. Do you know yourself
a vision veiled? What
the throat felt: need
clamping (his) / a forced
yield. It's a marvel,
scientifically speaking;
it will succumb
unhingingly. Whatever
wriggling resistance
I came with has been
quashed. The light
changed, a strange cloudy.
This I could turn or blank
but not pierce. His mad
rage—desire—dial me
to grunting always
crescendo. What can
naming solve now?
Call it, catalogue.
The stubborn cornice
and my stoppered ears.
Aren't we as hideous
as the most we have seen,
been done to? Not
if we don't remember.

Mania / He Said

Sugar, when I traffic your wholesome
flax, spend our twenty-one day visitation

eating fried restaurant eggs with bacon
and playing blackjack for sticks

of Fruit Stripe gum, harming
and scheming the next harm,

I need rotten redemption like the ravage
glaciers do to land. Sequined,

rhinestoned, I'll all night dance
at El Jardin, take a damsel home

to not marry, besmirch the domestic
that urges pure, sand my edges

round. There's not enough
rock and roll on this earth to swab

my eardrums filthy as I need
them. How many jangled weekends

packed with car-buying might this
require? When I hung a Bud Light sign

in the window of my basement
apartment on Racine, I was

flipping you the bird. Once
the party gets going, I can't hear

you knock over the din.

Vigil

and from the dark
and round the curve
a shoring up
a cupping air

I'm so afraid
I'll no breath wake
these nights should burn
stark lit-up day

a sun equipped
to corner find
and fill a house
an altar where

grandmothers come
line up votives
make a city
of one-inch flames

behold the floor
white and unchanged
the spreading spot
the pink-orange stain

I'll later scrub
my own thin blood
streaking the sink
he left me here

no shadow work
no buzzing fridge
one helpless room
a shade could haunt

Fragments, Effaced

In this story each body part plays itself. They come jagged. The heart's cortisol cocoon, a limbic wish. Race and race the veins. If this girl's eye— mine—catches his (cruel). It's my head hitting and hitting the chenille spread. His mad desire pinned me here. In his eye I read murder. Must not look there.

Bound and gagged five hours inside the tent. Lying in urine. What flashed. I know her.

This town is famous for my uncle who blew his brains into tree bark, there near the creek. Take a lesson. He may have saved his daughters decades of wordlessness. Not every death a tragedy.

That's my blood on the rag. Smudged on the door frame, thin in the watery sink. He has a knife. There's a word for this thing he does.

Ranch house, you disgust. You bricks will rot yourselves from inside into crab grass plot from sun from hatred: useless, silent mortar. Inside, I'm (she is) broken. Wrecked. Weren't the phone lines inviting, set to vibrate with sound but her frozen small hands.

Horror Mountain

you are   two rocks piled
roofless wall   less red
bib red bonnet   stare
sulfur's yellow ooze   denuded
hillside   you are stacked
armless stomachless   two
blank rocks   chin on shoulders
brick your mother birthed
baby   left to weather
remembered lost   child
grey grey nothing   clothes
turned rags no   sunshade no
wind break   you face where she
points you   no view   throw away
or press between   the mattress
like flowers like paper
blank blank   fake violets
wrap and sulfur greens   mothers
light incense   stone babies
lost and gone ones   your kept
sibling excels   maybe at chess
incense barely burns the day   cold
you are condemned   neckless
you are photo flat   a likeness
you live elsewhere or you don't
live   she can't have you
in your waking bareness
in your baby sweat song
she says good-bye   leaves
you freezing   if I had
arms   I'd straighten your bib
feed your stone   mouth until full

Manifest

Murderer, I'll belated tell it other ways.

Blood matted my hair, streaked my brow.

Every suffering the blank windows screened.

I wished to lift the roof off, show.

You weren't careful this once.

I was in no way angry.

I kept count by the tens into the hundreds.

The blood-soaked underwear a trophy.

Then: empty house; your strung-out odyssey.

Let's say I hung them on the mailbox at sunrise.

Subdivision peppered with brick cubes.

Maybe a neighbor at the door.

I don't answer her knock.

In my version, she doesn't give up.

Tenacity: calls the squad cars.

Imagine they respond to my clue.

Imagine they emergency me.

Unequivocal.

Punishable by electric chair.

Your blued and flaccid tongue a justice.

Let's say it/you/everything stops.

This version is my wish.

Prayer

Little lake
earth's thimble
glacial sink
take my ache
take the torn girl
the grieved woman
buoy her children
there where
the loon
calculates
its catch
where the
pickerel jumps
and the pocked
surface splits
or reflects
Black Mountain
I can't contain
all I've got
to carry let me
leave it to your
silt muck reeds
and granite
to your white
lilies and their
leeches to the
streams that
feed you deep
pond stay
close today
I'm counting
on your volume
your powers
to dilute to be

your gracious
self to ask no
questions pond
absorb receive
ripple then that
lovely silence
will you take
a few of these
troubles pond
and positively
drown them?

Seven Sins: A Warding

Prayer Against Sloth

No schooner sails this sound without its rope-burned crew. Mop scrub polish. I am the dry potted tree, weep the unwashed windowsill. I know industry when I see it. My house's prow needs paint. Braid or knit, turn something slack into. Help me to open this can, help me to chop this onion, help me to hold an idea still. Coil narrow scraps. Stuff my drafty windows full-woven till the red-brown mountain vagues. Make a spiral make a tower. Wrap. Products possess a use. My grandmother would have waxed this floor. I live one mile from a highway that's never empty. My porous table warps. Comb the children, show them how to hold their hands. Rest in this gauzy room while they play scales, middle to high C and back down.

Prayer Against Gluttony

Who would want to if I can bend to this fern where it was in the hollow now my tramp tramp yard. There are places to own to preserve side of a mountain and its glass wash your windows with the squeegee's long neck, brush the orange stucco painted wooden stairs. As much as you earn that's how much. Berkeley and its garden, a chiseled Czech cliff tramp tramp whistle. I've seen people lug their lunches up this high for the view for the ridged loll. Hate to mention hate to certain countries also ownable. I'm thinking of the way the earth takes a corpse over, its liquid jump-starting each body's bacteria. For a billion for the price of several thousand lives. The gun's crack saying leap outside your host organ and feed unless mummified. Bodies owned by microbes owned by earth a million trillion and within thirty years, not.

Prayer Against Envy

Sometimes a salt cellar and June air. What people have: electric fans, cherry desks. Everyone in the Place des Vosges wears red satin, all the vitrines boast olive drapes. Everyone in Agra sinks against her car: palms up, palms empty. Some own a lake's outline or fluted crystal. The salt clumped so she set the thing at the curb. How straw is hollow. Some keep score. When the kite twisted in a spruce. When the key slipped down a sewer. Sweep the porch bare of webs and sand and paint. See the festooned carriage pass: someone's baby, a likeness there's no word for, what she held. Latch the screen. I have nothing to give you. These two palms and the water between.

Prayer Against Anger

I like a taquería you can sit down at where they'll bring you a beer. Not so cold as the winters my daughters orphanaged. I'm stuck in this sentence, the object transitive: slam it to the pavement like quartz like a brick there's no aerie. Market hospital busy intersection. She had to but how could she: walk away. I do not allow as how. Of helmets, machine guns, riot gear, checkpoints: they're over-overreacting. I don't know bone shards blew. Restaurant. Know this body zipped into itself like a promise, advent-fragile. I always eat Chinese, chopsticks like crane legs. Thank you, Chairman Mao, for my flower petal girls. Fury more quilt square than flag. Daughters bookend. Waiting children Velcroed our knees in the orphanage hallway: take us too. Limited resources among the Tamil Tigers mean suicide bombers. Parse a body. Conjugate it.

Prayer Against Greed

How can I not unto fortune. This child walked from the forest. A shirt haloes the ribs and under. I haven't been to that bar where the dock was not satcheled not caramba how do you like your satay? At what hour can the grown-ups order Bloody Marys hungry. My friend said what if we gave way / to wanting: clean laundry, to not have broken be. I don't mean the day my heel took a nail: the foot intact in (gest). People are always flaunting their ultrasounds, feet of their babies. This child screamed two weeks and the adults. Confess to what. Plugged their ears, told her this is not rage. Can't. In this life. The chokecherry fruits it gnarls, August, purple, right on time. My face is made to watch it; they're holding me—holding me up / face this way / here, look—to the glass.

Prayer Against Pride

Dipped woman stained betel nut how did your back swell curve in rain. Under what load. I should not have loved nor thought my body finite. Ask me how old I am / this bucket / slow like a leaf at the zoo. Somebodiness sells. She can sit roadside that is from whence. She says I know the way and I know seeds. She's a valuable asset to her community. These thousand things: cars, cars, buffalo. The swinging bridge guarded both ends and the dogs don't listen except to rocks. Back to the germ: if I brag then my tenuous self will curl like burnt paper. I will arch, a simile. When people are six years old they might describe themselves as like-magnets. I'm sorry but the sky and its opening will.

Prayer Against Lust

No one's skin actually shines. Insert scenario. It's a bed or it's a trough. He did cocaine in high school or he built a house from mud. On my winter walk the pine cone looks like urge, the twigs like urge asleep. I'm too interested. A day counting out beads could solve, a week of counting: nuns' work. Skin not burnished either. Not on purpose I quicken but the roof. House roof, mouth roof. All things a lever: what five-second shiver can I attain, what thirty-year fixed ARM. Skin can swap one thing for its kin. Love poems end on an image, include the color blue.

Aubade

*The awful thing is that nothing is ever forgotten.
Then the child goes around with an absence of
confidence in things.*

from 'Home is Where We Start From'
D.W. Winnicott

Self-Portrait

Have you seen a girl about this high,
Mean rodeo presence?

Left her hours in the Lincoln to bake.
She flies in loops, kicks dirt.

Houses have insides and people
Admire and buy. Full of bowls.

I know my child's fingernail and earlobe.
Have you seen a girl about this high?

Milk teeth something else to part
With. The rodeo ring dusty. Barrel.

She's got a nub coming in: white
Turns pink where it shows through gum.

When the yay-high girl returns dusty
From her rodeo, accolades.

My girl grows new teeth in sleep.
Blue the room the underside of her bed.

Bowls are nice because they hold
Unkempt wanderings together chunk-like.

Urging the horse on: delicate. Think of
Dew, ride your horse like dew rides a bloom.

Wouldn't any little girl in this situation.
Ask for a better situation.

Put your arm in the bowl elbow-first and soak it.
Unutterables lodge in rafters.

Barrels white, a triangle, red stripes.
Clicking kisses with the upper throat: *go*.

I'm not asking for a room in which.
The horse is still the best conveyance I've known.

So much talk about bowls we forgot
To mention. I'll go back

Into the story and free the girl
Waiting for dinner in the dark apartment.

She will be surely split in sun in
Shadow. If he pressed harder just a little

On her throat. How close death was, how
Many times. No one has ever needed me more.

Cleft in the landscape if it's hilly.
There's room for beauty here; she's it.

About the Nanny who was Raped the Summer I Moved Here

Something amiss that June.
I was unpacking nesting bowls
sloughing their newspaper
like skin to my porch
when a mile away he
grabbed her, left
the child she cared for
fenced and squalling,
alarm that stunned my kitchen
silent. I read later
how the ranger heard the child,
how help dragged the bushes till
they found her hurt but alive.
Ten years ago now.
I know some ditches
and their slashing leaves,
the small of my back
where he pushed me, pinioned.
I've been the nanny
I've been the baby
in this stupid city,
my wish-away birth
accomplished,
my bleeding mother a baby too,
a hurt one and who wasn't?
That summer, the nanny's parents flew here,
thanked the ranger. In our rental,
my daughter turned two.
Nanny went back to school
in her native Sweden. I'm her pen pal:
her charge has grown into a red-faced
soccer fan. Memory is a funny thing.
Who can I thank who dragged me clear?

We write par avion. It's the almost-dieds.
Contorted: you can read it in our necks.
Did you break when they noticed?
I write her. Did someone help you
wash your legs? I write. I read about you.
A whole city palmed its outrage.
Her day was a day like this one:
I can't have another kind of June.
Chase a loiterer, Ranger. Patrol
the perimeter. I scare myself:
how I'm dabbing at my ragged
skin, my little hand a doll's. I knew
my mother's phone number but it
never occurred to me to call.

Woodland Nocturne

Trees like sentinels but they're naked.
You know when people escape camps and
Almost starve and walk across whole countries
To the border of another, sleeping by day? It's
Always in the forest they do this. Except once
I taught a boy who had walked across

The Sudan away from the ripping
And I don't think he encountered a single tree;
He never mentioned one. He could traverse
A rough continent, a twisting ocean, but the
Ripping sound followed him. You know
The Chinese dissident who survived on rat's

Hide, the one who wrote his book every night
And buried the manuscript in the garden
Before sun-up in case the police came? He said
Tree when he meant listen. One dawn, police did
Come and give chase. He flattened himself
First to one tree then the next. But a person

Is not the shape of a tree. There was prison time.
The manuscript was there when he
Dug it up. Changed. Today is a Saturday in March.
Also trees, also vigilance. I sit next to
My long-time husband and listen to
The scratchiness of yesterday's words.

This man I love doesn't smile. He reads
And the trees march the outside of my skin.
Next to us, a friendly iPhone couple
Checks the progress of a mid-east revolution,
Declares a dictator a stupid idiot. Japan will melt
Down and the UN strikes Libya from air. A girl

My daughter's age was dug from tsunami rubble;
She bowed to her rescuers and apologized
For the trouble she'd made. I apologize for the trouble
I've made and I hope the Libyans' roofs hold. Things
Are falling. Here's it's so quiet. Trees still stunned
By the record snowy winter, but the sun

Coaxing. We walked by the lake yesterday
And kicked humus, found brave peepers in a bog.
He says I haven't listened and I am craning now.
Recent events have severed parts of him, he says.
A year of asking blows like wind: it wasn't the thing
He wanted to tell me. That he didn't know a person

Could be nearly gnawed by his own disappointment.
Truth is, we're both nearly broken with grief.
On the train, I dream I'm crawling through
That forest. All my arms reach for him. At first
It's shadow or I might grab a uniformed gendarme,
Fatal mistake. But I won't give up my

Nighttime looking for the man whose tread
On the stair I know like my own, whose
Catch in the throat is my symphony.
I'm clever and I follow his markings I
Take the right trail I'm dogged
Careful in my devotion and when we are alone

I reach for his skin I've known these two decades
Trace a vein, back of his hand, open my mouth to say
And his sweet hands push and push and push
Me away until I learn exile anew and
Now there is no reason to run for cover
Except possibly for the children.

Benediction

Daughter, pack a beaver skin to wrap
yourself in. Daughter, bring

refreshment and jollity for your journey.
My love, tuck a ribbon in your hair

and this your great-grandmother's
comb. Daughter, men's ways

wax coarse. There are things
I have not told you of. Daughter,

you'll know the bloom of children soon,
each woman's heart and heart's ache.

Daughter, meat is done when it pushes
back against your finger. Oh love,

we live under the same moon. Daughter,
take this spoon to stir your sauce and take

my lantern for your piecework. I'll
be with you when you lullaby your babes

the words I sang you. Daughter,
go now and we'll each remember the other

smiling. Daughter, I'll visit when the snows
melt, when the mountain road clears,

daughter, my own, my very own, my heart,
I'll see you in the most and early spring.

Apology for an Incident after *The Sleeping Beauty*

Sweetie,
about that little café table
I almost shoved into your groin
on Amsterdam Avenue: our first
visit to Lincoln Center, the end
of the space-shuttle program,
stalemate in Congress, and our
doozy of six years. Sometimes I'm
more than I bargained for
but if you've got some good will left
can you toss it my way? Family
suicides aren't half as romantic
as Shakespeare would have them.
Touched, I am, but by my user father
who broke me early. Circles be
unbroken by and by and I'm
gluing this one to its very own
shore. But about that café table
and our future. Stalled for time,
I did. Ordered the fresh fruit
and it came riddled with grapefruit,
a no-go with my Xanax. What
was I yelling? Oh, it all seems
so long ago now, the ballerina
and her hundred-year snooze,
a whole kingdom afraid of sharp
things. I feared our return
to the borrowed apartment, so they
brought cappuccino, sniggered,
and I telegraphed to that eye-rolling
waitress, Girlfriend, someday you
might be fighting for your marriage
on an avenue at midnight too
so not so fast. Later we flossed

like to spit and fumed in separate rooms,
apartment too flimsy to hold us
or my memories. I thought I might
sleep on, I don't know, the countertop
or the fucking dinner table
or in this empty goddamn bathtub
but A, what I meant to say is actually:
my tired knees wish to bend in remorse,
they do. They and I want to say
we know what we've
put you through, jagged as I am
like a cursed girl in a world of spindles,
or maybe like a spindle and you're the girl:
we all need a shield from my cell's scramble,
my tongue's lash and really in my fury I just
outright love you.

To Stop Here

When people mention points of land
they say jut. Here a granite jaw line
into this tidal river. Stray from the path
and piles of empties bully me, distilled
to bright poison. Real tombstones
flank this meadow: one for the whole
family Fowle. To whom would I not
admit my desire to join them? Late fall,
Queen Anne's lace skeletons dry climb
my calves, ferry ticks. If I lie
among them. Redeem. Osprey mated
and done. This slope shows water
pocked with seals. The story revolves
around other characters, lost places,
but there's a you I miss. She
heavy-tugs me to this spot. How
otherwise to organize a day, devastation
like a plum? Tongue the inner stone. I've
presented this pretty scene to distract
and it does. Sharp glass under leaf
piles, haunted: someone's liquid ghost.
The you would arrive, if I wrote her in,
with hair streamers and a doughy lap.
Would plant anemones and cosmos
on my sill. I will lie down here till dusk
or past. A goldeneye motors by,
makes no call. Fabulous sun,
incorrigible weeds. They take over
and reclaim the road. A heart like a den
and who lives inside? If the you inhabits,
she'll knock around my chest, scuff the rug.
The day's not going anywhere. Stall:
I'll not move. I myself am hell.

Groundwater

Perhaps if I   near my father's
corpse right the town   where right
there. On the radio a   man confesses:
sleeps on his grandparents'   tomb
and cottonmouth   moccasins.
My grandparents   mean on diuretics
didn't notice. No one saw.
Wrangle my   hair onto pink foam rollers,
ride the barrels   for a ribbon a buckle
either/and   exotic to my Midwestern
Catholic girlfriends back   in the other life
to my   Texan relatives in this one.
Body of the father, pollute   my drinking
water: I'll absorb   you pre-filtration.
Snakes swim erstwhile   streets.
Radio   man says his grandparents
happy to have   him climb between:
Earl pull the sheets   up. I don't know
whose bed this   dark. Plainview, west
Texas. Time   passes. We bury
certain bodies   not their ghosts.
My great aunts   take the sacrament
tend the graves. Suicides,
delusionals: all our kin. My great
aunts   fail: their knees, a function.
Can   a body be sealed? How metal
is metal? How   slow is seep?

Street's Anatomy

Room wherein a clock's
red icing letters fall
back, room faces north
mountain. Also red. Thick-
lidded night. Either you're
awake or I am. You're the person
beyond which without whom
this window not soundproof.
We read, we study his/
hers declensions, we yawn,
your whiskers lengthen, we
flannel we classic we
halogen. This bed, my
daycared children, my gold
mini-van. Please measure
this house in hands. Spins
the tire, winter, remember
white drivewayed Honda
or the truck Joel bought
on Gulf veteran special,
oil inside earth
inside Q-mart. Oakland,
it's afternoon, sun a
template, remnant, after-
glow. My friend lives
there. One ocean, two
ocean. I can hear how a
tire on ice I can hear
distinct where the muskrat.
Want the park, want some stairs?
This bed my nexus. I ring her
on the portable. She doesn't
pick up she works with pinks
she soaks her brushes. I

tell her machine what organ
loss ate, my caged sweet-soft
innards. Afternoon, afternoon.
She paints the end of noise.
I love her machine. This has
nothing to do with you.

Aubade

In morning, the sink gathers and holds the moon-white
plate a daughter stacks there. Berry juice congeals.

Earth in morning turns like someone who hears
her name called, turns and lets the sun into her antechamber

then boudoir, the back hallway shut and dark. Shine
happens on the pond or its sandy skirt—ignites a piece of mica.

Napping raptors see it, one eye open: a glint, a movement,
a thirsty vole. If you don't occupy a hilltop and pause

in your wood splitting or in extracting a thorn from your foot—
if you don't look—the sun will sluice, change its angle, demote

the mica to stone. The plate shifts and the juice
congeals. She left it there and walked barefoot on the gray

carpet. I could run water. I could watch the hummingbird feeder
beyond streaked glass. It's noon and nearly dark, we're stuck

in the shadows, the day wanes and drains the counter/
threshold/pock-marked lawn of their blue like a corpse

with its veins tapped, pale and pale. The morning's promise
stalls where plain meets ridge, the way a closed mouth

haunts dark and contoured and only its owner knows the way
from tooth to tooth and down the supple throat.

Notes

The last sentence of 'To Stop Here' is Robert Lowell's.

Three lines in 'Evacuee' are Anne Carson's.

The phrase *some perfect year* of the book's title and 'Amnesiac's Journal' is Dickinson's.

'Horror Mountain' was inspired by a temple in rural Japan called Osore-zan (which means *Horror Mountain*). Osore-zan is located in a desolate valley near a sulfur spring and is dedicated to Jizo, a bodhisattva associated with the care of children. The temple consists of a central building and medicinal hot spring surrounded by many small shrines in honor of specific children who have died, were aborted or are missing; the children are represented by piled rock statues "dressed" in red cloths, often with a white bib added.

Acknowledgments

Grateful acknowledgment is made to the editors of the following magazines, in which some of these poems first appeared, sometimes in another form:

The Antioch Review: 'Greta Like a Plucked String'; *The Bakery*: 'Diurnal,' 'Invitation'; *The Drunken Boat*: 'Prayer Against Gluttony,' 'Prayer Against Greed,' 'Street's Anatomy' and 'To Stop Here' as 'Poem Ending with a Line by Robert Lowell'; *Green Mountains Review*: 'About the Nanny Who Was Raped the Summer I Moved Here'; *New Haven Review*: 'Fun with Dying'; *Phoebe*: 'Greta Gives Good Advice'; *The Poker*: '[flight 312]' and '[sketch]'; *River Styx*: 'Proverb'; *Spinoza Blue*: 'Compounded,' 'Telling,' 'Prayer'; *Toad*: 'Amnesiac's Journal'.

'Right to Remain' won the Lynda Hull Memorial Prize from *Crazyhorse* in 2005.

The Greta series was first published by In the First Place Press, New Haven, Connecticut, 2004, as *Many-Windowed House*. Additionally, several of these poems appeared in a chapbook entitled *Night, Relative to Day*, selected by Robert Pinsky and published by the Aldrich Museum of Contemporary Art, Ridgefield, Connecticut, in 2005. Eight of my poems were recorded and archived at The Knox Writers' House. Thank you to the Barbara Deming / Money for Women Fund which generously allowed time for the completion of this project.

I am grateful to the community of people who helped me complete this work. To my parents, John and Ann Gearen, thank you for supporting me and my family in millions of ways my whole life and for showing me that poetry is important; also, thanks to Sarah, Alejandra, John and Molly for help with the Tennessee residency. Thank you to my keen and generous first readers Suzanne (Norris) Heyd and Nancy Kuhl; they were among the Maine Women Writers, as were Rosemary Jones, Celia Lewis and Mindi Englart. Thank you to Lee and Tony Junker, especially for loan of their home for writing stints. To Diana Moller-Marino for folding my laundry and for friendship. Thank you to Nancy Meyer Lustman and Paula Ammerman. Thanks to Laura Hurwitz for daily writing perspective and support. To Tony Frazer at Shearsman for making this book a reality and for expert editing. To my students at ECA who reminded me every day how art can save lives. Too many friends to name have cheered me on during the writing of these poems. Thank you all for your love. You sustain me.

www.ingramcontent.com/pod-product-compliance
Lightning Source LLC
Chambersburg PA
CBHW020214090426
42734CB00008B/1065